HOME TEAM GEAR

Show your spirit with gear sporting your favorite team colors and mascot patches.

LEISURE ARTS, INC. • Maumelle, Arkansas

SCARF

EASY

SHOPPING LIST

Yarn (Medium Weight) MEDIUM 4

[5 ounces, 244 yards (141 grams, 223 meters)]:

- ☐ 1 skein self-striping yarn (each size)

Crochet Hook

- ☐ Size H (5 mm) **or** size needed for gauge

SIZE INFORMATION

Finished Measurements:

Small: 3½" wide x 59" long (9 cm x 150 cm)

Medium: 3½" wide x 63½" long (9 cm x 161.5 cm)

Large: 4¼" wide x 67½" long (11 cm x 171.5 cm)

Size Note: We have printed the instructions for the sizes in different colors to make it easier for you to find:

- · Size Small in Blue
- · Size Medium in Pink
- · Size Large in Green

Instructions in Black apply to all sizes.

GAUGE INFORMATION

14 sts = 4" (10 cm)

Gauge Swatch: 4" wide x 1¾" high (10 cm x 4.5 cm)

Ch 16.

Row 1: Dc in fourth ch from hook **(3 skipped chs count as first dc)** and in each ch across: 14 dc.

Row 2: Ch 1, turn; sc in each dc across.

Row 3: Ch 3 **(counts as first dc)**, turn; dc in next sc and in each sc across.

Rows 4 and 5: Repeat Rows 2 and 3.

Finish off.

INSTRUCTIONS

Ch 199{215-227}; place marker in second ch from hook for st placement.

Rnd 1 (Right side)**:** (2 Dc, ch 2, dc) in third ch from hook **(2 skipped chs count as first dc)**, dc in next ch and in each ch across to last ch, (dc, ch 2, 3 dc, ch 2, dc) in last ch; working in free loops of beginning ch *(Fig. 3, page 28)*, dc in each ch across to marked ch, ch 2; skip marked ch and join with slip st to next ch (first dc), remove marker: 400{432-456} dc and 4 ch-2 sps.

Rnd 2: Ch 1, sc in same st as joining and in each dc around working (sc, ch 2, sc) in each corner ch-2 sp; join with slip st to first sc: 408{440-464} sc and 4 ch-2 sps.

Rnd 3: Ch 3 **(counts as first dc)**, dc in next st and in each st around working (dc, ch 2, dc) in each corner ch-2 sp; join with slip st to first dc: 416{448-472} dc and 4 ch-2 sps.

Size Small & Size Medium Only

Rnds 4 and 5: Repeat Rnds 2 and 3: 432{464} dc and 4 ch-2 sps.

Finish off.

Size Large Only

Rnds 4 and 5: Repeat Rnds 2 and 3: 488 dc and 4 ch-2 sps.

Rnd 6: Repeat Rnd 3; finish off: 496 dc and 4 ch-2 sps.

EASY

SHOPPING LIST

Yarn (Medium Weight) MEDIUM 4

[7 ounces, 364 yards

(198 grams, 333 meters)]:

- ☐ Main Color - 1 skein
- ☐ Contrasting Color - 28 yards (25.5 meters)

Crochet Hook

- ☐ Size H (5 mm) **or** size needed for gauge

SIZE INFORMATION

Finished Measurements:

Small: 17" circumference x 6¾" high (43 cm x 17 cm)

Medium: 19" circumference x 7" high (48.5 cm x 18 cm)

Large: 20½" circumference x 8" high (52 cm x 20.5 cm)

Size Note: We have printed the instructions for the sizes in different colors to make it easier for you to find:

· Size Small in Blue

· Size Medium in Pink

· Size Large in Green

Instructions in Black apply to all sizes.

HAT

GAUGE INFORMATION

14 dc = 4" (10 cm),

7 rows/rnds = 3" (7.5 cm)

Gauge Swatch: 3" (7.5 cm) diameter

Work same as Crown through Rnd 3: 36 dc.

CROWN

Rnd 1 (Right side)**:** Using Main Color, make an adjustable loop to form a ring *(Figs. 1a-d, page 28)*; ch 3 **(counts as first dc, now and throughout)**, work 11 dc in ring; join with slip st to first dc: 12 dc.

Rnd 2: Ch 3, dc in same st as joining, 2 dc in next dc and in each dc around; join with slip st to first dc: 24 dc.

Rnd 3: Ch 3, 2 dc in next dc, (dc in next dc, 2 dc in next dc) around; join with slip st to first dc: 36 dc.

Rnd 4: Ch 3, dc in next dc, 2 dc in next dc, (dc in next 2 dc, 2 dc in next dc) around; join with slip st to first dc: 48 dc.

Rnd 5: Ch 3, dc in next 2 dc, 2 dc in next dc, (dc in next 3 dc, 2 dc in next dc) around; join with slip st to first dc: 60 dc.

Size Medium Only

Rnd 6: Ch 3, dc in next 8 dc, 2 dc in next dc, (dc in next 9 dc, 2 dc in next dc) around; join with slip st to first dc: 66 dc.

Size Large Only

Rnd 6: Ch 3, dc in next 3 dc, 2 dc in next dc, (dc in next 4 dc, 2 dc in next dc) around; join with slip st to first dc: 72 dc.

SIDES - All Sizes

Rnd 1: Ch 3, dc in next dc and in each dc around; join with slip st to first dc.

Repeat Rnd 1, 3{3-5} times.

Next Rnd: Ch 3, dc in next dc and in each dc around; drop Main Color, using Contrasting Color, join with slip st to first dc *(Fig. 4b, page 29)*, do **not** cut Main Color.

STRIPE

Rnd 1: Ch 3, dc in next dc and in each dc around; join with slip st to first dc.

Rnd 2: Ch 3, dc in next dc and in each dc around; cut Contrasting Color, using Main Color, join with slip st to first dc.

Repeat Rnd 1, 3 times; before joining last rnd, cut Main Color, using Contrasting Color, join with slip st to first dc.

Edging: Ch 1, sc in each dc around; join with slip st to first sc, finish off.

EASY

SHOPPING LIST

Yarn (Medium Weight) MEDIUM 4

Can Cozy

- ☐ Main Color - 35 yards (32 meters)
- ☐ Contrasting Color - 10 yards (9 meters)

Bottle Cozy

- ☐ Main Color - 45 yards (41 meters)
- ☐ Contrasting Color - 10 yards (9 meters)

Crochet Hook

- ☐ Size G (4 mm) or size needed for gauge

GAUGE INFORMATION

6 dc and 4 rnds = 1½" (3.75 cm)

Gauge Swatch: 2" (5 cm) diameter

Work same as Bottom: 30 sc.

The Can & Bottle Cozies are worked the same, only making the side of the Bottle Cozy longer than the Can Cozy.

CAN & BOTTLE COZIES

Finished Size: 7½" (19 cm) circumference

BOTTOM

Rnd 1 (Right side)**:** Using Main Color, make an adjustable loop to form a ring ***(Figs. 1a-d, page 28)***; work 6 sc in ring; do **not** join, place marker to indicate beginning of rnd ***(see Markers, page 28)***.

Rnd 2: 2 Sc in each sc around: 12 sc.

Rnd 3: (Sc in next sc, 2 sc in next sc) around: 18 sc.

Rnd 4: (Sc in next 2 sc, 2 sc in next sc) around: 24 sc.

Rnd 5: (Sc in next 3 sc, 2 sc in next sc) around; remove marker, slip st in Back Loop Only of next sc ***(Fig. 2, page 28)***: 30 sc.

SIDE

Rnd 1: Ch 2 **(counts as first dc, now and throughout)**, dc in Back Loop Only of next sc and each sc around; join with slip st to first dc.

Rnd 2: Ch 2, dc in both loops of next dc and each dc around; join with slip st to first dc.

Repeat Rnd 2, 2 times for Can Cozy and 4 times for Bottle Cozy.

Next Rnd: Ch 2, dc in next dc and in each dc around; drop Main Color, using Contrasting Color, join with slip st to first dc ***(Fig. 4b, page 29)***, do **not** cut Main Color.

STRIPE

Rnd 1: Ch 2, dc in next dc and in each dc around; join with slip st to first dc.

Rnd 2: Ch 2, dc in next dc and in each dc around; cut Contrasting Color, using Main Color, join with slip st to first dc.

Repeat Rnd 2 of Side, 3 times; before joining last rnd, cut Main Color, using Contrasting Color, join with slip st to first dc.

Edging: Ch 1, sc in each dc around; join with slip st to first sc, finish off.

EASY

SHOPPING LIST

Yarn (Medium Weight)

- ☐ Red - 12 yards (11 meters)
- ☐ Black - small amount
- ☐ Dark Orange - small amount
- ☐ White - small amount

Crochet Hook

- ☐ Size H (5 mm)
  or size needed for gauge

Additional Supplies

- ☐ Yarn Needle

GAUGE INFORMATION

Gauge Swatch: 2¼" (5.75 cm) diameter

Work same as Head: 24 dc.

CARDINAL PATCH

Finished Size: Approximately 3¼" (8.5 cm) wide

HEAD

Rnd 1 (Right side)**:** Using Red, make an adjustable loop to form a ring ***(Figs. 1a-d, page 28)***; ch 3 **(counts as first dc, now and throughout)**, work 11 dc in ring; join with slip st to first dc: 12 dc.

Note: Loop a short piece of yarn around any stitch to mark Rnd 1 as **right** side.

Rnd 2: Ch 3, dc in same st as joining, 2 dc in next dc and in each dc around; join with slip st to first dc, finish off (leave a long end if it will be sewn to a crocheted piece): 24 dc.

WING (Make 2)

UPPER SECTION

Rnd 1 (Right side)**:** Using Red, make an adjustable loop to form a ring; work 6 sc in ring; do **not** join, place marker to indicate beginning of rnd ***(see Markers, page 28)***.

Rnd 2: 2 Sc in each sc around: 12 sc.

Rnd 3: (Slip st, sc, slip st) in each of next 4 sc, leave remaining 8 sc unworked; finish off.

FEATHERS

Using Red, ch 6, sc in second ch from hook and in last 4 chs **(first Feather made)**, ★ ch 7, sc in second ch from hook and in last 5 chs; repeat from ★ 2 times **more**, ch 6, sc in second ch from hook and in last 4 chs; finish off leaving a long end for sewing: 5 Feathers.

Go, fight, Win!

Use Whipstitch ***(Fig. 6, page 29)*** for the method of sewing to join the pieces together.

Sew Feathers behind Upper Section, then tack the Feathers together. Sew the Wings to the Head.

FACE

Using Black, ch 3, 6 dc in third ch from hook; finish off leaving a long end for sewing.

FINISHING

Use photo as a guide for all finishing.

Sew Face to Head.

Using Dark Orange, embroider beak on Head using satin stitch ***(Figs. 8a & b, page 30)***.
Using White, embroider eyes and eyebrows using straight stitch ***(Fig. 7, page 30)***.
Using Red, add 2 small dots on beak using straight stitch.

CREST

With **right** side facing, join Red with sc in dc **before** center dc on top of Head ***(Figs. 5a & b, page 29)***; skip center dc, 2 dc in next dc; finish off.

EASY

SHOPPING LIST

Yarn (Medium Weight) MEDIUM 4

- ☐ Dark Brown - 12 yards (11 meters)
- ☐ White - small amount
- ☐ Yellow - small amount
- ☐ Black - small amount

Crochet Hook

- ☐ Size H (5 mm) **or** size needed for gauge

Additional Supplies

- ☐ Yarn Needle

GAUGE INFORMATION

Gauge Swatch: 2¼" (5.75 cm) diameter

Work same as Head: 24 dc.

EAGLE PATCH

Finished Size: Approximately 3¼" (8.5 cm) wide

HEAD

Rnd 1 (Right side)**:** Using White, make an adjustable loop to form a ring ***(Figs. 1a-d, page 28)***; ch 3 **(counts as first dc, now and throughout)**, work 11 dc in ring; join with slip st to first dc: 12 dc.

Note: Loop a short piece of yarn around any stitch to mark Rnd 1 as **right** side.

Rnd 2: Ch 3, dc in same st as joining, 2 dc in next dc and in each dc around; join with slip st to first dc, finish off (leave a long end if it will be sewn to a crocheted piece): 24 dc.

WING (Make 2)

UPPER SECTION

Rnd 1 (Right side)**:** Using Dark Brown, make an adjustable loop to form a ring; work 6 sc in ring; do **not** join, place marker to indicate beginning of rnd ***(see Markers, page 28)***.

Rnd 2: 2 Sc in each sc around: 12 sc.

Rnd 3: (Slip st, sc, slip st) in each of next 4 sc, leave remaining 8 sc unworked; finish off.

FEATHERS

Using Dark Brown, ch 6, sc in second ch from hook and in last 4 chs (**first Feather made**), ★ ch 7, sc in second ch from hook and in last 5 chs; repeat from ★ 2 times **more**, ch 6, sc in second ch from hook and in last 4 chs; finish off leaving a long end for sewing: 5 Feathers.

Use Whipstitch ***(Fig. 6, page 29)*** for the method of sewing to join the pieces together.

Sew Feathers behind Upper Section, then tack the Feathers together. Sew the Wings to the Head.

FINISHING

Use photo as a guide for all finishing.

Using Yellow, embroider beak on Head using satin stitch ***(Figs. 8a & b, page 30)***. Using Black, embroider eyes, eyebrows, and 2 small dots on beak using straight stitch ***(Fig. 7, page 30)***.

The Eagles refuse to lose!

EASY

SHOPPING LIST

Yarn (Medium Weight) 4

- ☐ Black - 12 yards (11 meters)
- ☐ Yellow - 12 yards (11 meters)
- ☐ White - small amount

Crochet Hook

- ☐ Size H (5 mm)
  or size needed for gauge

Additional Supplies

- ☐ Yarn Needle

GAUGE INFORMATION

Gauge Swatch: 2¾" (7 cm) diameter
Work same as Body: 36 dc.

We bring the sting!

HORNET PATCH

Finished Size: Approximately 3" (7.5 cm) wide

STITCH GUIDE

TREBLE CROCHET ***(abbreviated tr)***
YO twice, insert hook in st indicated, YO and pull up a loop (4 loops on hook), (YO and draw through 2 loops on hook) 3 times.

BODY

Rnd 1 (Right side)**:** Using Black, make an adjustable loop to form a ring ***(Figs. 1a-d, page 28)***; ch 3 **(counts as first dc, now and throughout)**, work 11 dc in ring; join with slip st to first dc: 12 dc.

Note: Loop a short piece of yarn around any stitch to mark Rnd 1 as **right** side.

Rnd 2: Ch 3, dc in same st as joining, 2 dc in each of next 9 dc, 2 tr in each of last 2 dc; join with slip st to first dc: 24 sts.

Rnd 3: Ch 3, 2 dc in next dc, (dc in next st, 2 dc in next st) around; join with slip st to first dc, finish off (leave a long end if it will be sewn to a crocheted piece): 36 dc.

HEAD

Rnd 1 (Right side)**:** Using Yellow, make an adjustable loop to form a ring; ch 3, work 11 dc in ring; join with slip st to first dc: 12 dc.

Rnd 2: Ch 3, dc in same st as joining, 2 dc in each of next 9 dc, 3 tr in each of last 2 dc; join with slip st to first dc, finish off leaving a long end for sewing: 26 sts.

ANTENNA

With **right** side facing, skip first 6 dc and join Black with sc around post of next dc; tightly ch 10; finish off and trim yarn close to chain.

Skipping next 6 dc, work second Antenna in same manner.

Use Whipstitch *(Fig. 6, page 29)* for the method of sewing to join the pieces together.

Using photo as a guide for placement, sew the Head to the Body placing the tr over the edge of the Body.

RIGHT WING

Rnd 1 (Right side)**:** Using White, ch 3, 5 dc in third ch from hook, ch 8; sc in second ch from hook and in next ch, hdc in next ch, dc in next ch, tr in last 3 chs; join with slip st to top of beginning ch-3.

Edging: 3 Sc in next dc, sc in next 2 dc, 3 sc in next dc, sc in last dc; working in free loops of ch-8 *(Fig. 3, page 28)*, sc in next 5 chs, 2 sc in next ch, sc in next ch; finish off leaving a long end for sewing.

LEFT WING

Using White and leaving a long end for sewing, ch 10.

Row 1 (Right side)**:** 5 Dc in third ch from hook, tr in next 3 chs, dc in next ch, hdc in next ch, sc in next ch, (sc, slip st, sc) in last ch.

Edging: Working in free loops of beginning ch, 2 sc in next ch, sc in next 5 chs, skip next 2 chs, sc in next ch, 3 sc in next dc, sc in next 2 dc, 3 sc in next dc, slip st in next dc; finish off.

LEG (Make 6)

Using Yellow, (ch 5 tightly, sc in second ch from hook) twice, ch 2; finish off.

FINISHING

Use photo as a guide for all finishing.

Sew the narrow end of the Wings to the Body, placing the Edging toward each other.

Sew 3 Legs to each side of the Body.

Using Black, embroider eyes using satin stitch *(Figs. 8a & b, page 30)*. Embroider lines using straight stitch *(Fig. 7, page 30)*.
Using White, add a small straight stitch on top of each eye.

BULLDOG PATCH

EASY

SHOPPING LIST

Yarn (Medium Weight) MEDIUM 4

- ☐ Light Grey - 12 yards (11 meters)
- ☐ Black - small amount
- ☐ White - small amount

Crochet Hook

- ☐ Size H (5 mm) **or** size needed for gauge

Additional Supplies

- ☐ Yarn Needle

GAUGE INFORMATION

Gauge Swatch: 3" (7.5 cm) diameter

Work same as Head: 36 dc.

Finished Size: Approximately 3" (7.5 cm) wide

STITCH GUIDE

TREBLE CROCHET ***(abbreviated tr)***

YO twice, insert hook in st indicated, YO and pull up a loop (4 loops on hook), (YO and draw through 2 loops on hook) 3 times.

HEAD

Rnd 1 (Right side)**:** Using Light Grey, make an adjustable loop to form a ring ***(Figs. 1a-d, page 28)***; ch 3 **(counts as first dc, now and throughout)**, work 11 dc in ring; join with slip st to first dc: 12 dc.

Note: Loop a short piece of yarn around any stitch to mark Rnd 1 as **right** side.

Rnd 2: Ch 3, dc in same st as joining, 2 dc in next dc and in each dc around; join with slip st to first dc: 24 dc.

Rnd 3: Ch 3, 2 dc in next dc, (dc in next dc, 2 dc in next dc) around; join with slip st to first dc, finish off (leave a long end if it will be sewn to a crocheted piece): 36 dc.

MUZZLE

Using Light Grey, ch 12.

Rnd 1 (Right side)**:** 6 Dc in third ch from hook, dc in next 8 chs, 7 dc in last ch; working in free loops of beginning ch ***(Fig. 3, page 28)***, dc in next 3 chs, sc in next 2 chs (bottom of Muzzle), dc in next 3 chs, skip next 2 chs; join with slip st to next ch, finish off leaving a long end for sewing.

Use Whipstitch ***(Fig. 6, page 29)*** for the method of sewing to join the pieces together.

Sew the Muzzle to the Head leaving 3 sts showing under the bottom of the Muzzle.

EAR (Make 2)

Using Light Grey, ch 6.

Row 1 (Right side)**:** Sc in second ch from hook, dc in next 2 chs, tr in last 2 chs; finish off leaving a long end for sewing.

FINISHING

Use photo as a guide for all finishing.

Sew end of row on Ears to **wrong** side of top of Head, 6 sts apart.

Using Black, embroider nose and eyes using satin stitch ***(Figs. 8a & b, page 30)***. Embroider mouth and eyebrows using straight stitch ***(Fig. 7, page 30)***. Using White, add a small straight stitch on top of each eye and also a small straight stitch on each side of mouth for teeth.

LION PATCH

Finished Size: Approximately 3" (7.5 cm) wide

EASY

SHOPPING LIST

Yarn (Medium Weight) 4

- ☐ Light Yellow - 12 yards (11 meters)
- ☐ Off White - small amount
- ☐ Dark Brown - small amount

(Bulky Weight Eyelash) 5

- ☐ Rust Eyelash - small amount

Crochet Hook

- ☐ Size H (5 mm) **or** size needed for gauge

Additional Supplies

- ☐ Yarn Needle

GAUGE INFORMATION

Gauge Swatch: 3" (7.5 cm) diameter (excluding fur)

Work same as Head: 36 dc.

Can't hide our Lion pride!

HEAD

Rnd 1 (Right side)**:** Using Light Yellow, make an adjustable loop to form a ring ***(Figs. 1a-d, page 28)***; ch 3 **(counts as first dc, now and throughout)**, work 11 dc in ring; join with slip st to first dc: 12 dc.

Note: Loop a short piece of yarn around any stitch to mark Rnd 1 as **right** side.

Rnd 2: Ch 3, dc in same st as joining, 2 dc in next dc and in each dc around; join with slip st to first dc: 24 dc.

Rnd 3: Ch 3, 2 dc in next dc, (dc in next dc, 2 dc in next dc) around; join with slip st to first dc, finish off (leave a long end if it will be sewn to a crocheted piece): 36 dc.

Fur: With **right** side facing, join Rust Eyelash yarn with sc in first dc ***(Figs. 5a & b, page 29)***; sc in next dc, 2 sc in next dc, (sc in next 2 dc, 2 sc in next dc) around; join with slip st to first sc, finish off.

LOWER JAW

Rnd 1 (Right side)**:** Using Off White, make an adjustable loop to form a ring; ch 3, work 11 dc in ring; join with slip st to first dc, finish off leaving a long end for sewing.

Use Whipstitch ***(Fig. 6, page 29)*** for the method of sewing to join the pieces together.

Using photo as a guide for placement, sew Lower Jaw to Head, placing edges together.

MUZZLE

Using Off White, ch 7.

Rnd 1 (Right side)**:** 5 Dc in third ch from hook, skip next ch, sc in next ch, skip next ch, 7 dc in last ch; working in unworked or free loops of beginning ch ***(Fig. 3, page 28)***, dc in next 3 chs, 2 dc in next ch, skip next ch; join with slip st to next ch, finish off leaving a long end for sewing.

Placing the Muzzle over the Lower Jaw, with both 7-dc groups positioned down, sew the Muzzle to the Head.

NOSE

Using Dark Brown, ch 4, (dc, ch 3, slip st) in fourth ch from hook; finish off leaving a long end for sewing.

Sew the Nose to the Muzzle.

EAR (Make 2)

Row 1: Using Light Yellow, ch 3, 6 dc in third ch from hook.

Row 2 (Right side)**:** Ch 1, turn; 2 sc in each dc across; finish off leaving a long end for sewing.

FINISHING

Use photo as a guide for all finishing.

Sew end of rows on Ears to **wrong** side of top of Head, 4 sts apart.

Using Dark Brown, embroider mouth using backstitch ***(Fig. 9, page 30)***. Embroider eyes above Muzzle using satin stitch ***(Figs. 8a & b, page 30)***. Embroider eyebrows using straight stitch ***(Fig. 7, page 30)***.
Using Off White, add a small straight stitch on top of each eye.

BOBCAT PATCH

EASY

SHOPPING LIST

Yarn (Medium Weight) MEDIUM 4

- ☐ Brown - 12 yards (11 meters)
- ☐ White - small amount
- ☐ Black - small amount
- ☐ Pink - small amount

(Bulky Weight Eyelash) BULKY 5

- ☐ White Eyelash - small amount
- ☐ Black Eyelash - small amount

Crochet Hook

- ☐ Size H (5 mm)
  or size needed for gauge

Additional Supplies

- ☐ Yarn Needle

GAUGE INFORMATION

Gauge Swatch: 3" (7.5 cm) diameter
Work same as Head: 36 dc.

Finished Size: Approximately 3" (7.5 cm) wide

HEAD

Rnd 1 (Right side)**:** Using Brown, make an adjustable loop to form a ring *(Figs. 1a-d, page 28)*; ch 3 **(counts as first dc, now and throughout)**, work 11 dc in ring; join with slip st to first dc: 12 dc.

Note: Loop a short piece of yarn around any stitch to mark Rnd 1 as **right** side.

Rnd 2: Ch 3, dc in same st as joining, 2 dc in next dc and in each dc around; join with slip st to first dc: 24 dc.

Rnd 3: Ch 3, 2 dc in next dc, (dc in next dc, 2 dc in next dc) around; join with slip st to first dc, finish off (leave a long end if it will be sewn to a crocheted piece): 36 dc.

FUR

First Side: With **right** side facing, skip joined dc and next dc, join White Eyelash yarn with sc in next dc *(Figs. 5a & b, page 29)*; sc in next 5 dc; finish off.

Second Side: With **right** side facing, skip next 20 dc and join White Eyelash yarn with sc in next dc; sc in next 5 dc; finish off.

LOWER JAW

Row 1 (Right side)**:** Using White, make an adjustable loop to form a ring; work 6 sc in ring; do **not** join, finish off leaving a long end for sewing.

Use Whipstitch *(Fig. 6, page 29)* for the method of sewing to join the pieces together.

Using photo as a guide for placement, sew Lower Jaw to Head, centering rounded edge between Fur.

MUZZLE

Using White, ch 7.

Rnd 1 (Right side)**:** 5 Dc in third ch from hook, skip next ch, sc in next ch, skip next ch, 7 dc in last ch; working in unworked or free loops of beginning ch ***(Fig. 3, page 28)***, dc in next 3 chs, 2 dc in next ch, skip next ch; join with slip st to next ch, finish off leaving a long end for sewing.

Placing the Muzzle over the straight edge of the Lower Jaw, with both 7-dc groups positioned down, sew the Muzzle to the Head.

EAR (Make 2)

Using Black, ch 4.

Row 1: Sc in second ch from hook, dc in last 2 chs: 3 sts.

Row 2 (Right side)**:** Turn; skip first dc, sc in last 2 sts; 3 sc in turning ch (top of Ear), working in free loops of beginning ch, sc in next 2 chs, slip st in last ch; finish off leaving a long end for sewing.

Fur: With **right** side facing, join Black Eyelash yarn with sc in center sc of 3-sc group at top of Ear; finish off.

FINISHING

Use photo as a guide for all finishing.

Sew end of rows on Ears to top of Head, 4 sts apart.

Using Pink, embroider nose on Muzzle using satin stitch ***(Figs. 8a & b, page 30)***.
Using White, embroider eyes using straight stitch ***(Fig. 7, page 30)*** and line on Ears using backstitch ***(Fig. 9, page 30)***.
Using Black, embroider mouth, stripes, and pupils using straight stitch.
Embroider whiskers using backstitch.

You're no match for the Bobcats!

EASY

SHOPPING LIST

Yarn (Medium Weight) MEDIUM 4

- ☐ Light Grey - 12 yards (11 meters)
- ☐ Grey - small amount
- ☐ White - small amount
- ☐ Black - small amount

(Bulky Weight Eyelash) BULKY 5

- ☐ White Eyelash - small amount

Crochet Hook

- ☐ Size H (5 mm) **or** size needed for gauge

Additional Supplies

- ☐ Yarn Needle

GAUGE INFORMATION

Gauge Swatch: 3" (7.5 cm) diameter
Work same as Head: 36 dc.

STITCH GUIDE

TREBLE CROCHET ***(abbreviated tr)***
YO twice, insert hook in st indicated, YO and pull up a loop (4 loops on hook), (YO and draw through 2 loops on hook) 3 times.

WOLF PATCH

Finished Size: Approximately 3" (7.5 cm) wide

HEAD

Rnd 1 (Right side)**:** Using Light Grey, make an adjustable loop to form a ring ***(Figs. 1a-d, page 28)***; ch 3 **(counts as first dc, now and throughout)**, work 11 dc in ring; join with slip st to first dc: 12 dc.

Note: Loop a short piece of yarn around any stitch to mark Rnd 1 as **right** side.

Rnd 2: Ch 3, dc in same st as joining, 2 dc in next dc and in each dc around; join with slip st to first dc: 24 dc.

Rnd 3: Ch 3, (2 dc in next dc, dc in next dc) 4 times, 2 dc in next dc changing to Grey in last dc made ***(Fig. 4a, page 29)***, cut Light Grey, (dc in next dc, 2 dc in next dc) 7 times; join with slip st to first dc, finish off (leave a long end if it will be sewn to a crocheted piece): 36 dc.

Fur: With **right** side facing, join White Eyelash yarn with sc in first Light Grey dc ***(Figs. 5a & b, page 29)***; sc in next dc, 2 sc in next dc, (sc in next 2 dc, 2 sc in next dc) 4 times; finish off.

LOWER JAW

Rnd 1 (Right side)**:** Using White, make an adjustable loop to form a ring; ch 3, work 10 dc in ring; join with slip st to first dc, finish off leaving a long end for sewing.

Use Whipstitch ***(Fig. 6, page 29)*** for the method of sewing to join the pieces together.

Using photo as a guide for placement, sew the top half of the Lower Jaw to the edge of the Head, centering it over the Fur and allowing the bottom to hang over the edge.

MUZZLE

Using White, ch 7.

Rnd 1 (Right side)**:** 5 Dc in third ch from hook, skip next ch, sc in next ch, skip next ch, 7 dc in last ch; working in unworked or free loops of beginning ch *(Fig. 3, page 28)*, dc in next ch, place marker in last dc made for st placement, dc in next 2 chs, 2 dc in next ch, skip next ch; join with slip st to next ch, finish off leaving a long end for sewing.

The Wolves lead the pack!

PATCH

Row 1: With **right** side of Muzzle facing and working in Back Loops Only, join Grey with sc in marked dc, remove marker; sc in next 2 dc: 3 sc.

Row 2: Ch 1, turn; sc in each sc across.

Row 3: Ch 2, turn; sc in second ch from hook and in next 2 sc, 2 sc in last sc: 5 sc.

Row 4: Ch 1, turn; sc in each sc across.

Row 5: Ch 1, turn; sc in first sc, skip next sc, 6 dc in next sc, skip next sc, sc in last sc; finish off leaving a long end for sewing: 8 sts.

Placing the Muzzle over half of the Lower Jaw and using matching colors, sew the upper portion of the Muzzle and the Patch to the Head.

LEFT EAR

Using White, ch 6.

Row 1 (Right side)**:** Sc in second ch from hook, dc in next 2 chs, tr in last 2 chs; finish off: 5 sts.

Row 2: With **right** side facing, join Grey with slip st in ch at base of first sc; sc in same st, 2 sc in first sc, sc in last 4 sts; finish off leaving a long end for sewing.

RIGHT EAR

Work same as Left Ear through Row 1.

Row 2: With **right** side facing and working in free loops of beginning ch, join Grey with sc in first ch; sc in next 3 chs, 2 sc in next ch, (sc, slip st) in first sc; finish off leaving a long end for sewing.

FINISHING

Use photo as a guide for all finishing.

Sew end of rows on Ears to **wrong** side of top of Head, placing them 5 sts apart with the Grey sts toward center.

Using Black, embroider nose and eyes using satin stitch *(Figs. 8a & b, page 30)*. Embroider mouth and eyebrows using straight stitch *(Fig. 7, page 30)*.
Using White, add a small straight stitch on top of each eye.

EASY

TIGER PATCH

Finished Size: Approximately 3" (7.5 cm) wide

SHOPPING LIST

Yarn (Medium Weight) 4

- ☐ Orange - 12 yards (11 meters)
- ☐ White - small amount
- ☐ Black - small amount

(Bulky Weight Eyelash) 5

- ☐ White Eyelash - small amount

Crochet Hook

- ☐ Size H (5 mm) **or** size needed for gauge

Additional Supplies

- ☐ Yarn Needle

GAUGE INFORMATION

Gauge Swatch: 3" (7.5 cm) diameter
Work same as Head: 36 dc.

HEAD

Rnd 1 (Right side)**:** Using Orange, make an adjustable loop to form a ring *(Figs. 1a-d, page 28)*; ch 3 **(counts as first dc, now and throughout)**, work 11 dc in ring; join with slip st to first dc: 12 dc.

Note: Loop a short piece of yarn around any stitch to mark Rnd 1 as **right** side.

Rnd 2: Ch 3, dc in same st as joining, 2 dc in next dc and in each dc around; join with slip st to first dc: 24 dc.

Rnd 3: Ch 3, 2 dc in next dc, (dc in next dc, 2 dc in next dc) around; join with slip st to first dc, finish off (leave a long end if it will be sewn to a crocheted piece): 36 dc.

FUR

First Side: With **right** side facing, skip joined dc and next dc, join White Eyelash yarn with sc in next dc *(Figs. 5a & b, page 29)*; sc in next 5 dc; finish off.

Second Side: With **right** side facing, skip next 20 dc and join White Eyelash yarn with sc in next dc; sc in next 5 dc; finish off.

LOWER JAW

Row 1 (Right side)**:** Using White, make an adjustable loop to form a ring; work 6 sc in ring; do **not** join, finish off leaving a long end for sewing.

Use Whipstitch *(Fig. 6, page 29)* for the method of sewing to join the pieces together.

Using photo as a guide for placement, sew Lower Jaw to Head, centering rounded edge between Fur.

MUZZLE

Using White, ch 7.

Rnd 1 (Right side)**:** 5 Dc in third ch from hook, skip next ch, sc in next ch, skip next ch, 7 dc in last ch; working in unworked or free loops of beginning ch ***(Fig. 3, page 28)***, dc in next 3 chs, 2 dc in next ch, skip next ch; join with slip st to next ch, finish off leaving a long end for sewing.

Placing the Muzzle over the straight edge of the Lower Jaw, with both 7-dc groups positioned down, sew the Muzzle to the Head.

EAR (Make 2)

Using Black, ch 4.

Row 1: Sc in second ch from hook, dc in last 2 chs: 3 sts.

Row 2 (Right side)**:** Turn; skip first dc, sc in last 2 sts; 3 sc in turning ch, working in free loops of beginning ch, sc in next 2 chs, slip st in last ch; finish off leaving a long end for sewing.

Welcome to the Tiger Nation!

FINISHING

Use photo as a guide for all finishing.

Sew end of rows on Ears to **wrong** side of top of Head, 6 sts apart.

Using Black, embroider nose on Muzzle using satin stitch ***(Figs. 8a & b, page 30)*** and eyes above Muzzle. Embroider mouth and stripes using straight stitch ***(Fig. 7, page 30)***.
Using White, embroider line on Ears using backstitch ***(Fig. 9, page 30)***; add a small straight stitch on top of each eye.

EASY

SHOPPING LIST

Yarn (Medium Weight) MEDIUM 4

- ☐ Brown - 12 yards (11 meters)
- ☐ Tan - small amount
- ☐ Black - small amount
- ☐ White - small amount

Crochet Hook

- ☐ Size H (5 mm) **or** size needed for gauge

Additional Supplies

- ☐ Yarn Needle

GAUGE INFORMATION

Gauge Swatch: 3" (7.5 cm) diameter
Work same as Head: 36 dc.

BEAR PATCH

Finished Size: Approximately 3" (7.5 cm) wide

HEAD

Rnd 1 (Right side)**:** Using Brown, make an adjustable loop to form a ring ***(Figs. 1a-d, page 28)***; ch 3 **(counts as first dc, now and throughout)**, work 11 dc in ring; join with slip st to first dc: 12 dc.

Note: Loop a short piece of yarn around any stitch to mark Rnd 1 as **right** side.

Rnd 2: Ch 3, dc in same st as joining, 2 dc in next dc and in each dc around; join with slip st to first dc: 24 dc.

Rnd 3: Ch 3, 2 dc in next dc, (dc in next dc, 2 dc in next dc) around; join with slip st to first dc, finish off (leave a long end if it will be sewn to a crocheted piece): 36 dc.

LOWER JAW

Rnd 1 (Right side)**:** Using Tan, make an adjustable loop to form a ring; ch 3, work 11 dc in ring; join with slip st to first dc, finish off leaving a long end for sewing.

Use Whipstitch ***(Fig. 6, page 29)*** for the method of sewing to join the pieces together.

Using photo as a guide for placement, sew Lower Jaw to Head, placing edges together.

with a
Cool Blues

MUZZLE

Using Tan, ch 7.

Rnd 1 (Right side)**:** 5 Dc in third ch from hook, skip next ch, sc in next ch, skip next ch, 7 dc in last ch; working in unworked or free loops of beginning ch ***(Fig. 3, page 28)***, dc in next 3 chs, 2 dc in next ch, skip next ch; join with slip st to next ch, finish off leaving a long end for sewing.

Placing the Muzzle over the Lower Jaw, with both 7-dc groups positioned down, sew the Muzzle to the Head.

NOSE

Using Black, ch 4, (dc, ch 3, slip st) in fourth ch from hook; finish off leaving a long end for sewing.

Sew the Nose to the Muzzle.

EAR (Make 2)

Row 1: Using Brown, ch 3, 6 dc in third ch from hook.

Row 2 (Right side)**:** Ch 1, turn; 2 sc in each dc across; finish off leaving a long end for sewing.

FINISHING

Use photo as a guide for all finishing.

Sew end of rows on Ears to **wrong** side of top of Head, 3 sts apart.

Using Black, embroider mouth using backstitch ***(Fig. 9, page 30)***. Embroider eyes above Muzzle using satin stitch ***(Figs. 8a & b, page 30)***. Embroider eyebrows using straight stitch ***(Fig. 7, page 30)***.
Using White, add a small straight stitch on top of each eye.

Don't you dare mess with the Bears!

GENERAL INSTRUCTIONS

ABBREVIATIONS

ch(s)	chain(s)
cm	centimeters
dc	double crochet(s)
hdc	half double crochet(s)
mm	millimeters
Rnd(s)	Round(s)
sc	single crochet(s)
sp(s)	space(s)
st(s)	stitch(es)
tr	treble crochet(s)
YO	yarn over

CROCHET TERMINOLOGY		
UNITED STATES		INTERNATIONAL
slip stitch (slip st)	=	single crochet (sc)
single crochet (sc)	=	double crochet (dc)
half double crochet (hdc)	=	half treble crochet (htr)
double crochet (dc)	=	treble crochet (tr)
treble crochet (tr)	=	double treble crochet (dtr)
double treble crochet (dtr)	=	triple treble crochet (ttr)
triple treble crochet (tr tr)	=	quadruple treble crochet (qtr)
skip	=	miss

GAUGE

Exact gauge is **essential** for proper size. Before beginning your project, make the sample swatch given in the individual instructions in the yarn and hook specified. After completing the swatch, measure it, counting your stitches and rows carefully. If your swatch is larger or smaller than specified, **make another, changing hook size to get the correct gauge.** Keep trying until you find the size hook that will give you the specified gauge.

SYMBOLS & TERMS

★ — work instructions following ★ as many **more** times as indicated in addition to the first time.

( ) or **[ ]** — work enclosed instructions **as many** times as specified by the number immediately following **or** work all enclosed instructions in the stitch or space indicated **or** contains explanatory remarks.

colon (:) — the number(s) given after a colon at the end of a row or round denote(s) the number of stitches or spaces you should have on that row or round.

Yarn Weight Symbol & Names	LACE 0	SUPER FINE 1	FINE 2	LIGHT 3	MEDIUM 4	BULKY 5	SUPER BULKY 6	JUMBO 7
Type of Yarns in Category	Fingering, size 10 crochet thread	Sock, Fingering, Baby	Sport, Baby	DK, Light Worsted	Worsted, Afghan, Aran	Chunky, Craft, Rug	Super Bulky, Roving	Jumbo, Roving
Crochet Gauge* Ranges in Single Crochet to 4" (10 cm)	32-42 sts**	21-32 sts	16-20 sts	12-17 sts	11-14 sts	8-11 sts	6-9 sts	5 sts and fewer
Advised Hook Size Range	Steel*** 6 to 8, Regular hook B-1	B-1 to E-4	E-4 to 7	7 to I-9	I-9 to K-10½	K-10½ to M/N-13	M/N-13 to Q	Q and larger

*GUIDELINES ONLY: The chart above reflects the most commonly used gauges and hook sizes for specific yarn categories.

** Lace weight yarns are usually crocheted with larger hooks to create lacy openwork patterns. Accordingly, a gauge range is difficult to determine. Always follow the gauge stated in your pattern.

*** Steel crochet hooks are sized differently from regular hooks–the higher the number, the smaller the hook, which is the reverse of regular hook sizing.

CROCHET HOOKS																	
U.S.	B-1	C-2	D-3	E-4	F-5	G-6	7	H-8	I-9	J-10	K-10½	L-11	M/N-13	N/P-15	P/Q	Q	S
Metric - mm	2.25	2.75	3.25	3.5	3.75	4	4.5	5	5.5	6	6.5	8	9	10	15	16	19

ADJUSTABLE LOOP

Wind the yarn around two fingers to form a ring ***(Fig. 1a)***, slide the yarn off your fingers and grasp the strands at the top of the ring ***(Fig. 1b)***. Insert the hook from **front** to **back** into the ring, pull up a loop, YO and draw through the loop on hook to lock the ring ***(Fig. 1c)***.

Working around **both** strands, work stitches in the ring as specified, then pull the yarn end to close ***(Fig. 1d)***.

Fig. 1a

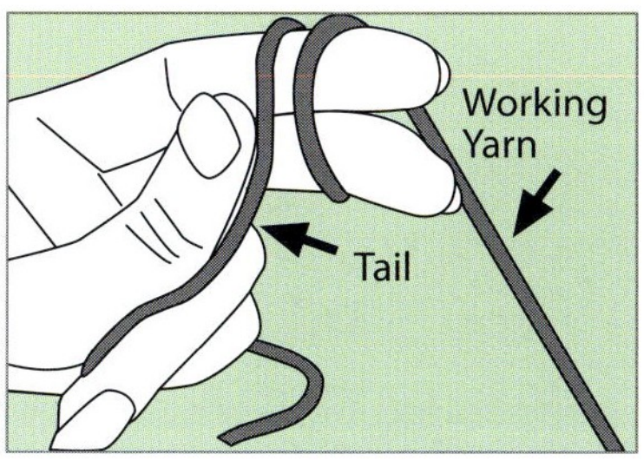

Fig. 1b

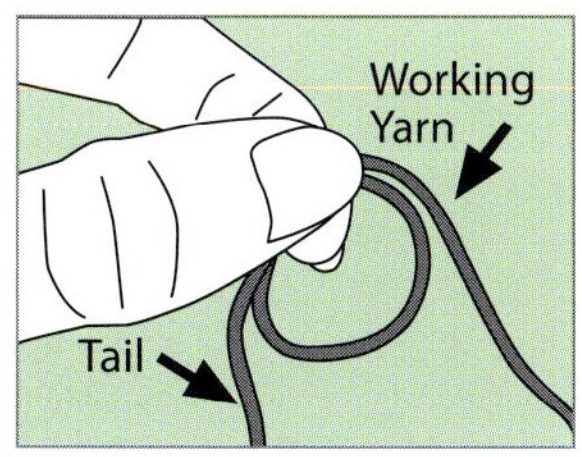

Fig. 1c

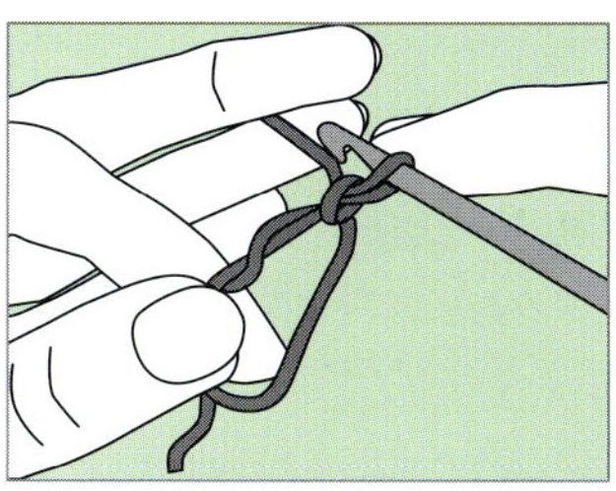

Fig. 1d

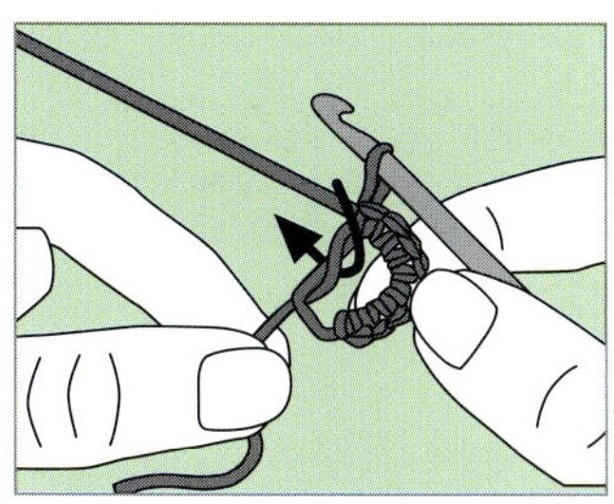

BEGINNER	Projects for first-time crocheters using basic stitches. Minimal shaping.
EASY	Projects using yarn with basic stitches, repetitive stitch patterns, simple color changes, and simple shaping and finishing.
INTERMEDIATE	Projects using a variety of techniques, such as basic lace patterns or color patterns, mid-level shaping and finishing.
EXPERIENCED	Projects with intricate stitch patterns, techniques and dimension, such as non-repeating patterns, multi-color techniques, fine threads, small hooks, detailed shaping and refined finishing.

MARKERS

Markers are used to help distinguish the beginning of each round being worked. Place a 2" (5 cm) scrap piece of yarn before the first stitch of each round, moving the marker after each round is complete.

BACK LOOP ONLY

Work only in loop(s) indicated by arrow ***(Fig. 2)***.

Fig. 2

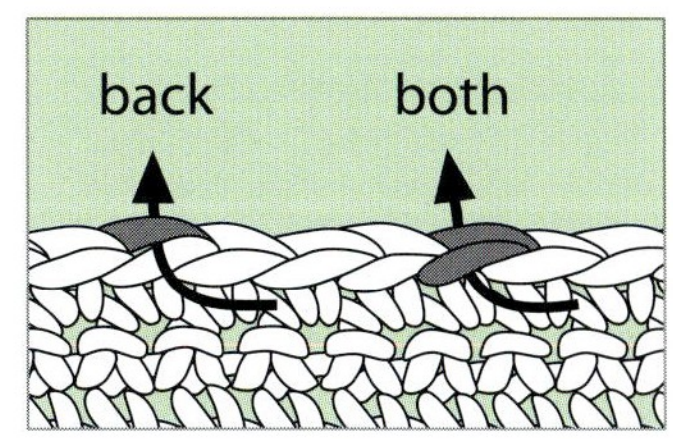

FREE LOOPS OF A CHAIN

When instructed to work in free loops of a chain, work in loop indicated by arrow ***(Fig. 3)***.

Fig. 3

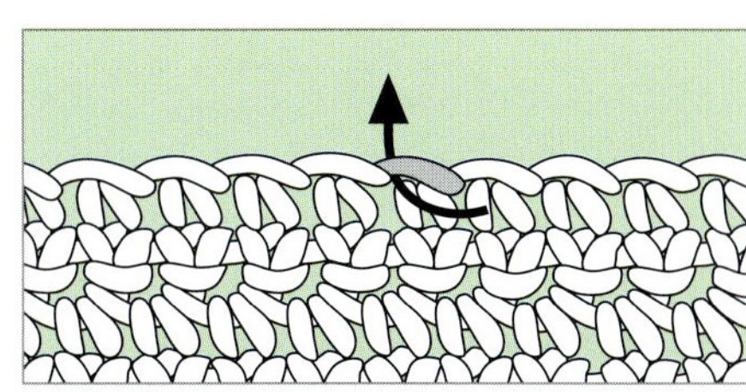

CHANGING COLORS

To change colors while working a dc, YO, insert hook in stitch indicated, YO and pull up a loop, YO and draw through 2 loops on hook, drop yarn, with new yarn *(Fig. 4a)*, YO and draw through 2 loops on hook.

Fig. 4a

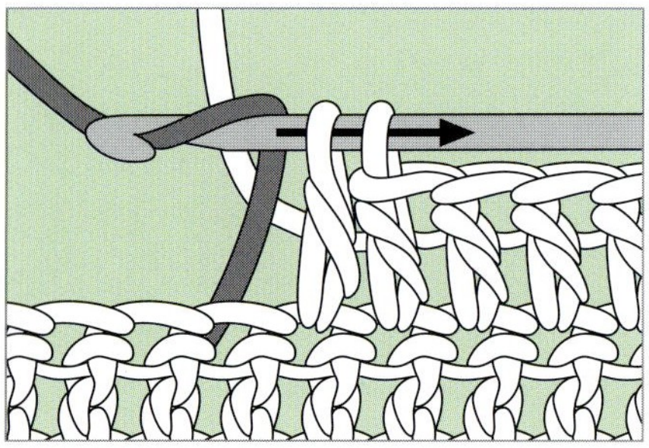

To change colors while joining with slip st, drop yarn, insert hook in first st *(Fig. 4b)*, hook new yarn and draw through st **and** loop on hook.

Fig. 4b

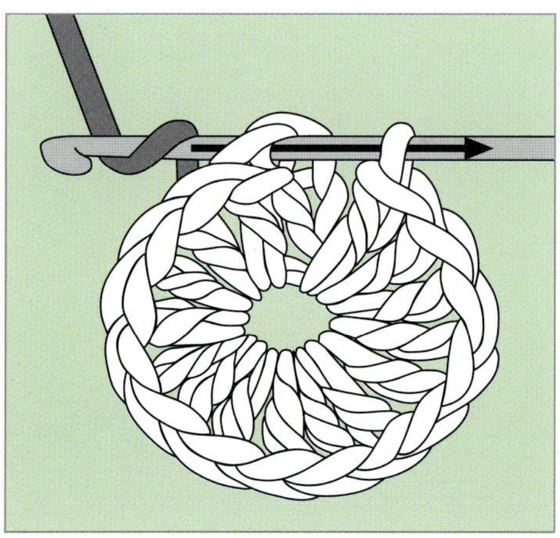

JOINING WITH SC

When instructed to join with sc, begin with a slip knot on hook. Insert hook in stitch indicated, YO and pull up a loop, YO and draw through both loops on hook *(Figs. 5a & b)*.

Fig. 5a

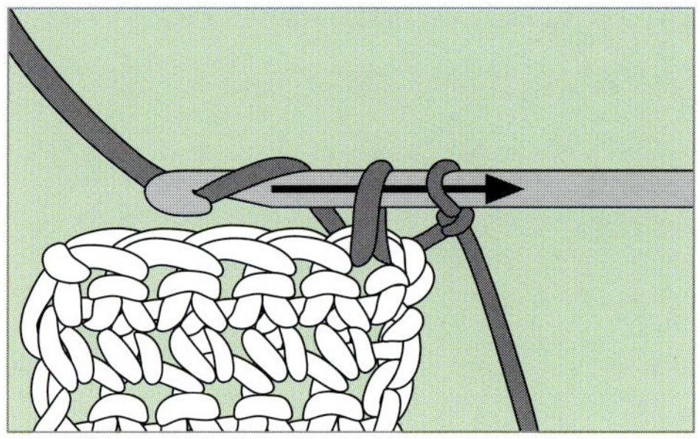

Fig. 5b

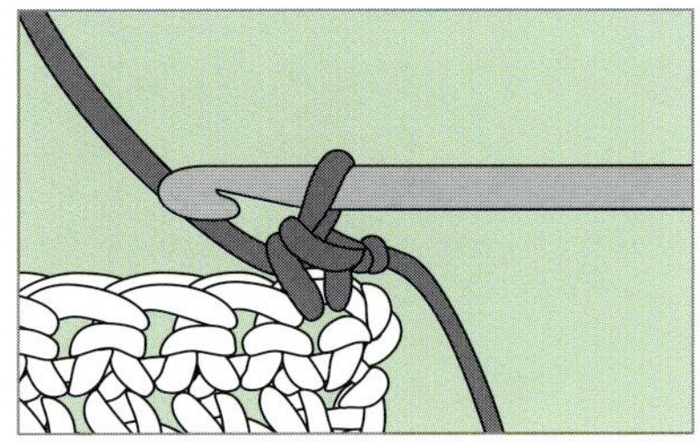

WHIPSTITCH

To sew a piece to another, insert the needle from **front** to **back** through two strands of a stitch or end of a row on the top piece, then through a stitch on the bottom piece *(Fig. 6)*. Bring the needle around and insert it through the next strands on the piece, then through a stitch. Continue working in same manner.

Fig. 6

Watch our technique videos made just for you!
www.LeisureArts.com/6695

EMBROIDERY STITCHES

STRAIGHT STITCH

Straight stitch is just what the name implies, a single, straight stitch. Come up at 1 and go down at 2 *(Fig. 7)*.

Fig. 7

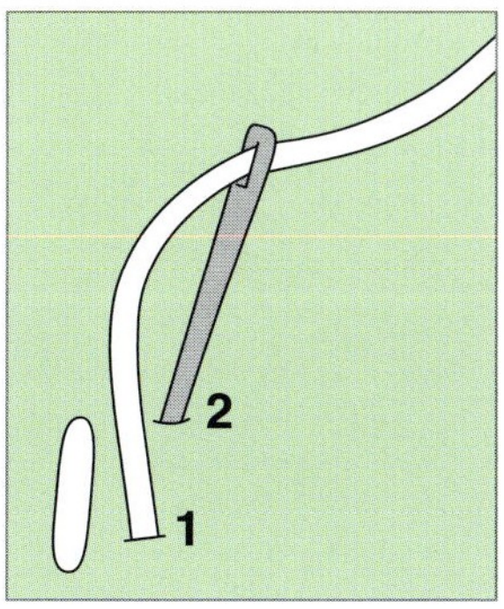

SATIN STITCH

Satin stitch is a series of straight stitches worked side-by-side that touch but do not overlap *(Fig. 8a)* **or** come out of and go into the same stitch *(Fig. 8b)*. Come up at odd numbers and go down at even numbers.

Fig. 8a

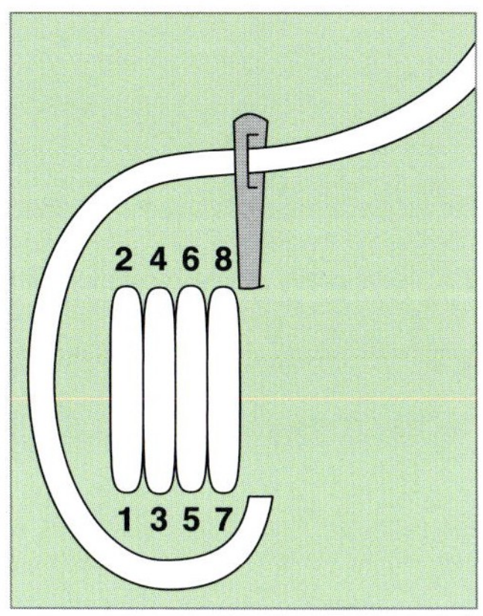

Fig. 8b

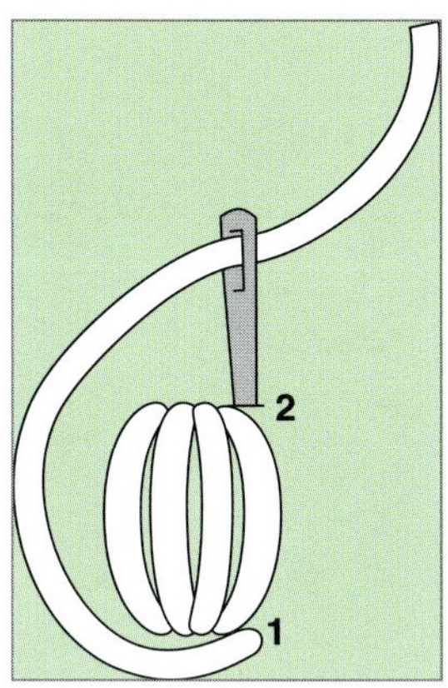

BACKSTITCH

The backstitch is worked from **right** to **left**. Come up at 1, go down at 2 and come up at 3 *(Fig. 9)*. The second stitch is made by going down at 1 and coming up at 4.

Fig. 9

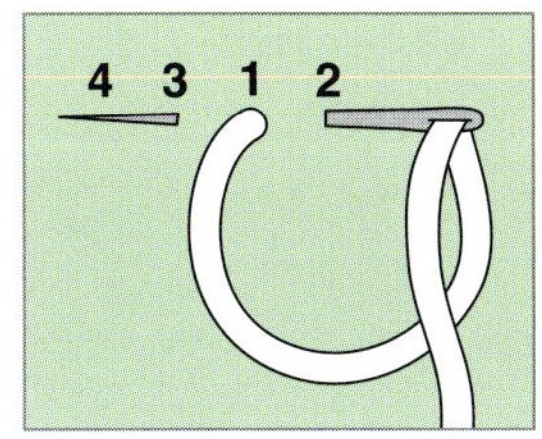

YARN INFORMATION

The items in this book were made using medium weight yarn. A Bulky Weight Eyelash yarn was also used as fur. Any brand of yarn may be used. It is best to refer to the yardage/meters when determining how many skeins or balls to purchase. Remember, to arrive at the finished size, it is the GAUGE/TENSION that is important, not the brand of yarn.

For your convenience, listed below are the yarns used to create our photography models. Because yarn manufacturers make frequent changes in their product lines, you may sometimes find it necessary to use a substitute yarn or to search for the discontinued product at alternate suppliers (locally or online).

SCARF
Red Heart® Team Spirit™
Small - #0948 Green/Gold
Medium - #0935 Navy/White
Large - #0952 Red/Black

HAT
Red Heart® Super Saver®
Small
Main Color - #0389 Hunter Green
Contrasting Color - #0321 Gold
Medium
Main Color - #0387 Soft Navy
Contrasting Color - #0311 White
Large
Main Color - #0319 Cherry Red
Contrasting Color - #0312 Black

CAN COZY
Red Heart® Super Saver®
Main Color - #0389 Hunter Green
Contrasting Color - #0321 Gold

BOTTLE COZY
Red Heart® Super Saver®
Main Color - #0319 Cherry Red
Contrasting Color - #0312 Black

PATCHES
CARDINAL
Red Heart® Super Saver®
Red - #0319 Cherry Red
Black - #0312 Black
Dark Orange - #0256 Carrot
White - #0311 White

EAGLE
Red Heart® Super Saver®
Dark Brown - #0365 Coffee
White - #0311 White
Yellow - #0324 Bright Yellow
Black - #0312 Black

HORNET
Red Heart® Super Saver®
Black - #0312 Black
Yellow - #0324 Bright Yellow
White - #0311 White

BULLDOG
Red Heart® Super Saver®
Light Grey - #0341 Light Grey
Black - #0312 Black
White - #0311 White

LION
Red Heart® Super Saver®
Light Yellow - #0320 Cornmeal
Off White - #0316 Soft White
Dark Brown - #0365 Coffee
Lion Brand® Fun Fur®
Rust Eyelash - #135 Terracotta

BOBCAT
Red Heart® Super Saver®
Brown - #0336 Warm Brown
White - #0311 White
Black - #0312 Black
Pink - #0706 Perfect Pink
Lion Brand® Fun Fur®
White Eyelash - #100 White
Black Eyelash - #153 Black

WOLF
Red Heart® Super Saver®
Light Grey - #0341 Light Grey
Grey - #0400 Grey Heather
White - #0311 White
Black - #0312 Black
Lion Brand® Fun Fur®
White Eyelash - #100 White

TIGER
Red Heart® Super Saver®
Orange - #0254 Pumpkin
White - #0311 White
Black - #0312 Black
Lion Brand® Fun Fur®
White Eyelash - #100 White

BEAR
Red Heart® Super Saver®
Brown - #0336 Warm Brown
Tan - #0334 Buff
Black - #0312 Black
White - #0311 White

Meet the Designer:

JESSICA BOYER

Jessica Boyer learned to crochet in childhood, taught by her grandmother, but she started crocheting more after she was diagnosed with fibromyalgia in her early twenties. "I like to make amigurumi animals that look semi-realistic and playful," she said. "This is definitely a passion for me, from sketching to crocheting to assembling the pieces."

High school sculptural work and college classes in graphic design have come in handy, she says. "I always work the amigurumi pieces more as I would a soft sculpture. I sketch some quick ideas of what I want the subject to look like, and then I look at as many photos as I possibly can of what I want to make and at every angle possible."

A stay-at-home mom, Jessica loves "cheesy" horror movies, reading, and '90s alternative music. Other arts and crafts that she enjoys are cross stitch, wire jewelry making, and acrylic painting. More of her designs for Leisure Arts can be found in *Spirit Animals* (#6458) and *Farm Animals* (#75429). She also is on Ravelry.com and Etsy.com and blogs at http://jessboyercrochet.tumblr.com.

We have made every effort to ensure that these instructions are accurate and complete. We cannot, however, be responsible for human error, typographical mistakes, or variations in individual work.

Production Team: Instructional/Technical Writer - Cathy Hardy; Editorial Writer - Susan Frantz Wiles; Senior Graphic Artist - Lora Puls; Graphic Artist - Victoria Temple; Photo Stylists - Sondra Daniel and Angela Alexander; and Photographers - Ken West and Jason Masters.